ULTIMATE STRATEGY

HOW TO WRITE A ONE PAGE STRATEGIC BUSINESS PLAN

By Norman David Roussell, MBA

ISBN-13: 978-1516971824
ISBN-10: 1516971825

ULTIMATE STRATEGY
HOW TO WRITE A ONE PAGE STRATEGIC BUSINESS PLAN

Table of Contents

Table of Contents (Cont'd)

A Message from the Author

Draw upon **FAITH** to conquer fear.
"Fear knocked on the door and faith answered. No one was there."
Old English Proverb

Demonstrate **PERSEVERANCE** to scorn idleness.
"By perseverance the snail reached the Ark."
Charles Spurgeon

Embody **FORTITUDE** to overcome weakness.
*"As a camel beareth labor, and heat, and hunger, and thirst,
through deserts of sand, and fainteth not;
so the fortitude of a man shall sustain him through all perils."*
Egyptian Pharaoh Akhenaton

Embrace **HOPE** to purge cynicism and pessimism.
"Learn from yesterday, live for today and hope for tomorrow."
Albert Einstein

Display **PATIENCE** in the face of irritation or annoyance.
"Patience is the companion of wisdom."
Saint Augustine

Faith. Perseverance. Fortitude. Hope. Patience.
I am an entrepreneur!

- Norman David Roussell, MBA

ULTIMATE STRATEGY
HOW TO WRITE A ONE PAGE STRATEGIC BUSINESS PLAN

What is Strategic Business Planning?

Strategic business planning is the process of defining the direction of your company and how you will allocate resources to achieve business success. Strategic business planning is action-driven planning that focuses on the ENTREPRENEURIAL EFFORT required to build a successful company.

ENTREPRENEURIAL EFFORT (def.)
The use of intelligence, education and skills, along with perseverance, faith and fortitude to innovatively or creatively implement an idea to start or grow a business regardless of the potential obstacles and challenges to success.

ENTREPRENEURIAL EFFORT FORMULA[1]

Owner

Team

$$\sum [(IQ + EQ + SQ) \times (InCrQ^2)] \times [(Pv + Ft + Fd)] + [(HR+CR+TR)]$$

Formula Component	Definition
Intelligence (IQ)	Capacity for learning
Education (EQ)	Acquisition of knowledge gained through formal or informal instruction or training
Skill (SQ)	The ability to do something well
Innovation and Creativity (InCrQ)	Something new or different that transcends traditional ideas, rules or patterns
Perseverance (Pv)	Steady persistence in a course of action or purpose
Faith (Ft)	Unyielding belief in something without proof of its existence or possibility
Fortitude (Fd)	Mental or emotional strength in the face of difficulty or adversity
Human Resources (HR)	Number of people/team members available to help achieve success
Capital Resources (CR)	Amount of capital available to achieve success
Time Resources (TR)	Amount of time available to achieve success

A company's development of a new application for tablet PCs is an example of entrepreneurial effort.

The process of aligning the resources to coordinate, plan and execute the launch of a new application for tablet PCs is an example of strategic business planning.

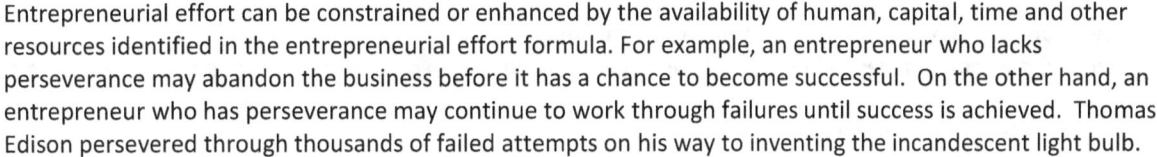

Entrepreneurial effort can be constrained or enhanced by the availability of human, capital, time and other resources identified in the entrepreneurial effort formula. For example, an entrepreneur who lacks perseverance may abandon the business before it has a chance to become successful. On the other hand, an entrepreneur who has perseverance may continue to work through failures until success is achieved. Thomas Edison persevered through thousands of failed attempts on his way to inventing the incandescent light bulb.

"Many of life's failures are experienced by people who did not realize how close they were to success when they gave up."
- Thomas Edison

---

[1] Developed by the author.

Strategic business planning occurs at three levels within every business, regardless of its size. Whether you operate a small home-based business or a multi-national conglomerate, those levels include:

THE BUSINESS LEVEL
What type of business do you operate?
For example, manufacturing, distribution, service, or retail

THE COMPETITIVE LEVEL
How does your business compete?
For example, globally, nationally, regionally or locally

THE FUNCTIONAL LEVEL
How do you synchronize your resources to maximize outcomes?
For example, creating daily assignments for team members

Taking the time to develop a formal one page strategic business plan is simply a more effective way of doing something that you are already doing in your business every day.

Why Do You Need a One Page Strategic Business Plan?

A one page strategic business plan helps you jump-start the business planning process and it helps you:

Maximize the use of limited resources
For example, in a small firm, the owner may have to balance his or her day between being the CEO, the receptionist and the janitor.

Focus the company's entrepreneurial efforts
For example, if your team has several great ideas, a strategic business plan can help them focus on the ideas that best fit the company's vision.

Clarify roles and responsibilities within your company
Clearly defined roles improve accountability within your company.

Gain BUY-IN from your employees, clients, suppliers and investors
Buy-in is essential for the long-term growth and sustainability of every company.

Capitalize on new and emerging trends to grow your company
For example, adding a Facebook® page or creating a blog as a part of your social media marketing strategy is an example of how to capitalize on new or emerging trends to grow your company.

Identify value-added opportunities to grow your company
For example, if you are an electrician you can partner with a plumber to provide value-added services for clients.

Attract capital to grow your company
You can use your one page strategic business plan in conjunction with a loan application or investment proposal to secure capital for your business.

> ✓ *Maximize resources*
> ✓ *Focus efforts*
> ✓ *Clarify roles*
> ✓ *Gain buy-in*
> ✓ *Capitalize on trends*
> ✓ *Identify opportunities*
> ✓ *Attract capital*
> ✓ *Realize your vision*

BUY-IN *(def.)*
Agreement with or commitment to a plan or idea.

Ultimately, you need a one page strategic business plan to help you realize your company's vision.

ULTIMATE STRATEGY
HOW TO WRITE A ONE PAGE STRATEGIC BUSINESS PLAN

What is Your Big Idea?

*"There are many pathways to success, but only one beginning...
An idea backed by a burning desire to achieve it."*

- Norman David Roussell

Strategic business planning begins with an idea- your idea for starting and growing a business. Unfortunately, every idea is **not a good idea for a business**. What are the characteristics of a good idea for a business?

A good idea for a business...

- ✓ solves a problem for consumers
- ✓ is new or unique
- ✓ is an improvement to an existing product or service
- ✓ appeals to a mass market or to a NICHE MARKET
- ✓ can generate a profit

LENNY'S LAWNCARE & CHICKEN WINGS

NICHE MARKET *(def.)*
Specific segment of a larger group or market.

If your idea is an improvement to a product or service that already exists, learn as much as you can about the market to determine how you can position your product or service for success in the marketplace.

If your idea is new or unique, test it in the marketplace to learn what works and what doesn't work with consumers before you invest in a full-scale product or service launch.

Think about your idea:

1. What problem does it solve for your potential customers?
2. Is your idea new or unique?
3. Is your idea an improvement to an existing product or service?
4. Does your idea appeal to a mass market?
5. Does your idea appeal to a niche market?
6. Can you earn a profit from your idea?

Tip! Use the internet and libraries to research your idea. Ask friends and colleagues for their opinions about your idea to gain additional insight about your chances for success.

Assignment #1: Write Down Your Big Idea

On the following pages, answer the six (6) questions above and then write down your idea in a clear and concise statement using no more than a single paragraph.

Big Idea Worksheets

Briefly describe how your idea solves a problem for consumers.

_____

_____

_____

_____

_____

_____

Briefly describe how your idea is new, unique or an improvement to an existing product or service.

_____

_____

_____

_____

_____

_____

Briefly describe whether your idea appeals to a mass market or to a niche market.

_____

_____

_____

_____

_____

_____

Briefly describe how your business will generate a profit.

_____

_____

_____

_____

_____

_____

My Big Idea

_____

_____

_____

_____

_____

_____

_____

_____

_____

_____

_____

_____

_____

_____

Your idea is the first step towards successful strategic business planning.

Developing Your Company's Business Model

Once you have formulated your business idea, you need to develop your **business model.**

A business model describes the rationale for how an organization creates, delivers and captures value.[2]

CREATING VALUE

A business creates value through a "win-win" proposition. Customers win by receiving a product or service they want or need and the business wins by selling its product or service at a price that can generate a profit. Successful restaurants create value by offering consumers great food at reasonable prices.

DELIVERING VALUE

A business delivers value in a variety of ways: *Price, quality, quantity, service and reliability to name a few.* How your company delivers value will impact consumer perception about your company which will, in turn, impact your company's bottom line either positively or negatively. Retail giants Walmart® and Target® let consumers know how they deliver value through their slogans, "Save money, live better," and "Expect more, pay less," respectively.

CAPTURING VALUE

A business captures value by transforming a product or service into its monetary equivalent. For example, Facebook® captured value from its free social networking site by charging companies a fee to advertise to Facebook's® one billion active monthly users.

PLAYERS AND PARTNERS

In addition to determining how your business will create, deliver and capture value, you need to identify the "players and partners", like your suppliers, employees, manufacturers and distributors, who will help you create, deliver and capture value for your customers.

Assignment #2: Develop Your Company's Business Model

On the following pages, identify the "players and partners" that impact your business model and briefly describe the roles they play for your company. Next, write down how your business will create, deliver and capture value for your customers.

---

[2] *Osterwalder, A. and Pigneur, Y., **Business Model Generation: A Handbook for Visionaries, Game Changers and Challengers,** Wiley (2010).*

Business Model Worksheets

Players and Partners

TYPE: S = Supplier; **TP** = Teaming Partner; **JV** = Joint Venture Partner; **M** = Manufacturer;
W = Wholesale Distribution Channel; **R** = Retail Distribution Channel; **C** = Client/Consumer; **O** = Other

_____

_____

_____

_____

_____

_____

_____

_____

My business creates value by....

_____

_____

_____

_____

_____

_____

_____

_____

_____

My business delivers value by...

_____

_____

_____

_____

_____

_____

_____

_____

My business captures value by...

_____

_____

_____

_____

_____

_____

_____

_____

_____

_____

My Company's Business Model

_____

_____

_____

_____

_____

_____

_____

_____

_____

_____

_____

_____

_____

_____

_____

_____

_____

_____

_____

Developing your business model is the second step
towards successful strategic business planning.

Your Company's Master Mind Group

Author Napoleon Hill first introduced the concept of the "Master Mind" in his book, *"Think & Grow Rich"*. In the book, Napoleon Hill defined the Master Mind as the ***"Coordination of knowledge and effort, in a spirit of harmony, between two or more people, for the attainment of a definite purpose."***

Through your Master Mind group, you will gain feedback and guidance from experts who have specialized knowledge to help you avoid some of the pitfalls and roadblocks to success. You will also benefit from a SYNERGY of efforts that will help you maximize your company's limited resources.

The individuals that comprise your Master Mind group should include, at a minimum, your:

SYNERGY (def.)
Result generated from the interaction amongst a group of individuals where the whole is greater than the sum of the parts.

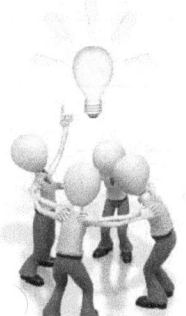

- Accountant or CPA
- Attorney
- Business Banker
- Insurance Consultant
- Risk Management Consultant
- Human Resource Consultant
- Business Mentor

Industrialist Andrew Carnegie attributed his entire fortune to the power he accumulated through the Master Mind principle.

Entrepreneur Henry Ford used the Master Mind principle to help launch the industrial revolution when he invented the assembly line manufacturing process.

Andrew Carnegie
1835-1919

Henry Ford
1863-1947

"Analyze the record of any man who has accumulated a great fortune and you will find that he has either consciously or unconsciously employed the Master Mind principle."

- Napoleon Hill

Assignment #3: Assemble Your Master Mind Group

Identify the individuals you would like to have as members of your Master Mind group. Write down their qualifications, skills and the resources you hope to benefit from by having them as members of your Master Mind group. If you must, ask friends and colleagues for assistance in finding individuals who can help you build your company through the Master Mind principle.

Master Mind Group Worksheets

(Member: Name and Master Mind Group Role)

Member _____

Qualifications/Skills/Resources_____

_____

Member _____

Qualifications/Skills/Resources_____

_____

Member _____

Qualifications/Skills/Resources_____

_____

Member _____

Qualifications/Skills/Resources_____

_____

Member _____

Qualifications/Skills/Resources_____

_____

Member _____

Qualifications/Skills/Resources_____

_____

ULTIMATE STRATEGY
How to Write a One Page Strategic Business Plan

Member _____

Qualifications/Skills/Resources_____

_____

Member _____

Qualifications/Skills/Resources_____

_____

Member _____

Qualifications/Skills/Resources_____

_____

Member _____

Qualifications/Skills/Resources_____

_____

Member _____

Qualifications/Skills/Resources_____

_____

Member _____

Qualifications/Skills/Resources_____

_____

My Company's Master Mind Group

Tip! The number of members in your Master Mind group is up to you. The goal of the Master Mind group is to ensure you have the professional expertise you need to advise you on building a successful company.

(Name, Title and Role)

_____

_____

_____

_____

_____

_____

_____

_____

_____

_____

Alternate(s)

_____

_____

_____

_____

_____

Assembling a Master Mind group is the third step
towards successful strategic business planning.

Components of a One Page Strategic Business Plan

A one page strategic business plan contains the following elements:

- Mission Statement
- Vision Statement
- Values Statement
- SWOT/Competitive Analysis
- Objectives
- Critical Success Factors
- Strategies
- Prioritized Action Plan

Mission Statement

*Your company's **MISSION STATEMENT** is a statement of intent that should convey to the reader in a clear and concise manner why your company exists. Your mission statement helps your company operate within its CORE COMPETENCY for the benefit of your employees, customers, suppliers, bankers or investors.*

The mission statement should capture the essence of your organization and should answer the following questions:

CORE COMPETENCY *(def.)*
Something a company does really well that gives it a competitive advantaged.

1. Why does your company exist?
2. What products/services does your company provide?
3. Why will customers buy from your company?
4. What is your company committed to providing to customers?

Sample Mission Statement #1
Our mission is to develop quality products that provide our clients with the best widget value on the market.

Sample Mission Statement #2
Our company is dedicated to creating products and services that help entrepreneurs gain greater access to capital and credit so they can build competitively viable businesses.

Assignment #4: Develop Your Company's Mission Statement

Use the next few pages to answer the four mission statement (4) questions above on the way to finalizing your company's mission statement. If you already have a mission statement, review it to see if you need to update or improve it. Perform an internet search for 'mission statements' for additional guidance and examples of mission statements.

Mission Statement Worksheets

Tip! Refer to your idea and business model as you prepare your mission statement.

My company exists to...

_____

_____

_____

_____

_____

_____

My company provides "?" products and/or services.

_____

_____

_____

_____

_____

_____

Customers will buy from my company because....

_____

_____

_____

_____

_____

_____

My company is committed to providing customers...

_____

_____

_____

_____

_____

_____

My Company's Mission Statement

_____

_____

_____

_____

_____

_____

_____

_____

_____

_____

_____

_____

_____

_____

_____

_____

Creating a mission statement is the fourth step in successful strategic business planning.

Vision Statement

*Your company's **VISION STATEMENT** is an idealized view of what you want your company to be in the future. Your vision statement is the driving force behind every business objective and business strategy you establish for your company.*

Your vision statement describes to the reader what type of company you plan to build over time. Effective vision statements need not be long, but must clearly answer some or all of these questions:

1. What type of company are you building? [For example, retail, wholesale or service]

2. What market does your company serve? [For example, global, national, regional or local]

3. Who are your target clients? [For example, businesses or individuals]

4. How large will your company become? [For example, annual revenue or units sold]

5. When will your company achieve its vision? [For example, in months or years]

Sample Vision Statement #1
Our vision is to be the preferred widget supplier to widget retailers in North America.

Sample Vision Statement #2
Within the first two years of operations, grow ABC Company into a $50 million dollar publishing company serving colleges and universities around the world.

Assignment #5: Develop Your Company's Vision Statement

Answer the questions below to develop your vision statement based on the criteria above. If you already have a vision statement, review it to see if you need to update or improve it.

Vision Statement Worksheet

1. My company is a _____ company.

2. My company operates _____.

3. My company's target clients include _____

   _____.

4. My company's monthly, quarterly or annual sales goal is _____.

5. My company will achieve its vision in _____ months or years.

My Company's Vision Statement

_____

_____

_____

_____

_____

_____

_____

_____

_____

_____

_____

_____

_____

_____

Creating a vision statement is the fifth step towards successful strategic business planning.

Values Statement

*Your company's **VALUES STATEMENT** informs the public how your company treats its clients, employees, suppliers and members of the communities in which it operates.*

Your values are the guiding principles, the standards of conduct which govern how your company operates. Your values should convey your company's commitment to operating ethically, honestly, respectfully and responsibly.

Your leadership, along with your company values, set the tone for your company's culture. To develop your values statement, answer the following questions:

1. What values are important to you as the company's founder, owner or CEO?

2. What values are important to your team?

3. What values are important in your industry?

4. What values are important in the communities in which you operate?

Sample Values Statement #1
Ethical, honest, respectful and responsible are the values by which we operate. As a result, we will engage in no transaction that does not benefit all parties involved.

Sample Values Statement#2
ABC Company is committed to acting honestly and ethically in all our transactions and dealings. We are committed to treating our employees, clients, and suppliers fairly and respectfully and we are dedicated to acting responsibly in the communities in which we work.

Assignment #6: Develop Your Company's Values Statement

Use the following pages to develop your company values statement. If you already have a company values statement, review it to determine if it needs updating or improvement.

Values Statement Worksheets

What values are important to you as the company's founder, owner or CEO?

_____

_____

_____

_____

_____

_____

_____

What values are important to your team?

_____

_____

_____

_____

_____

_____

_____

What values are important in your industry?

_____

_____

_____

_____

_____

_____

_____

What values are important in the communities in which you operate?

_____

_____

_____

_____

_____

_____

_____

My Company's Values Statement

_____

_____

_____

_____

_____

_____

_____

_____

_____

_____

_____

_____

_____

_____

_____

_____

_____

_____

_____

_____

Creating a company values statement is the sixth step towards
successful strategic business planning.

SWOT Analysis

*Also known as a competitive or situational analysis, a **SWOT ANALYSIS** examines the internal strengths and weaknesses of an organization and the external opportunities and threats it faces. A good SWOT Analysis can be used to help craft strategies that capitalize on the company's strengths and opportunities and develop solutions to combat the company's weaknesses and threats.*

COMPANY CAPABILITIES: *AN ANALYSIS OF YOUR COMPANY'S INTERNAL **S**TRENGTHS AND **W**EAKNESSES*

An OBJECTIVE ANALYSIS of your company's strengths and weaknesses reveals how well your company is operating with its current human, capital, time and other resources. It can also compares your company to similar companies in your target market or the best companies in the industry to determine where you company fits in the marketplace.

OBJECTIVE ANALYSIS *(def.)*
Analysis based on fact, not opinions or feelings.

ENVIRONMENTAL FACTORS: *AN ANALYSIS OF YOUR COMPANY'S EXTERNAL **O**PPORTUNITIES AND **T**HREATS*

An external analysis of your company's opportunities and threats reveals how your company is affected by its competitors, suppliers, clients and other external factors that are out of your control like rising fuel costs.

Q:

STRENGTHS	WEAKNESSES
What makes your company great?	What is holding your company back?
OPPORTUNITIES	**THREATS**
What can make your company better?	What can impede or derail your success?

A:

STRENGTHS	WEAKNESSES
- Management team - Innovative products	- Marketing strategy - Limited capital
OPPORTUNITIES	**THREATS**
- Global distribution - Joint ventures	- Rising energy costs - Political unrest in foreign markets

SWOT Analysis and the Malcolm Baldrige National Quality Award

The *Malcolm Baldrige National Quality Award* is given by the President of the United States to businesses that apply and are judged to be outstanding in seven areas:

Leadership: Examines how senior executives guide the organization and how the organization addresses its responsibilities to the public and practices good citizenship.

Strategic Planning: Examines how the organization sets strategic directions and how it determines key action plans.

Customer Focus: Examines how the organization determines requirements and expectations of its customers.

Measurement, Analysis and Knowledge Management: Examines the management, effective use, analysis and improvement of data and information to support key organization processes and the organization's performance management system.

Workforce Focus: Examines how the organization enables its workforce to develop its full potential and how the workforce is aligned with the organization's objectives.

Operations Focus: Examines aspects of how key production/delivery and support processes are designed, managed and improved.

Results: Examines the organization's performance and improvement in its key business areas:

- Customer satisfaction;
- Financial and marketplace performance;
- human resources;
- supplier and partner performance;
- operational performance; and
- Organizational performance relative to competitors.

> **Learn more about how the Baldrige Program can help improve the competiveness and performance of your organization @ www.nist.gov/Baldrige/**

Assess your company's strengths, weaknesses, opportunities and threats based, in part, on the areas established for the Malcolm Baldrige National Quality Award.

Assignment #7: Perform a SWOT Analysis

Perform a SWOT Analysis of your company by evaluating your strengths, weaknesses, opportunities and threats.

SWOT Analysis Worksheets

Strengths

_____

_____

_____

_____

_____

_____

_____

_____

Weaknesses

_____

_____

_____

_____

_____

_____

_____

_____

_____

_____

Opportunities

Threats

Company SWOT Analysis

You do not have to fill in every space, but you can add spaces if necessary. Tip! Include weaknesses and threats in a plan used as a management document (an internal plan). Remove weaknesses and threats from a plan presented to banks or investors (an external plan).

STRENGTHS	WEAKNESSES

OPPORTUNITIES	THREATS

Assessing your company's strengths, weakness, opportunities and threats is the seventh step towards successful strategic business planning.

Objectives

*When you state goals so that they are specific, measurable, attainable, realistic and timed they are called **OBJECTIVES.***

An objective is a specific outcome you want to achieve. Objectives can be short-term, mid-term or long-term.

- Most short-term objectives are outcomes you hope to achieve in less than 90 days;

- Most mid-term objectives are outcomes you hope to achieve in less than 12-months; and

- Most long-term objectives are outcomes you hope to achieve in 12-months or longer.

Your vision statement is the ultimate long-term objective.

Effective objectives should contain three key elements:

1. An observable and measurable goal;

2. The conditions under which the goal is achieved; and

3. The time frame for achieving the goal.

Sample Objectives

FISCAL YEAR (FY) *(def.)*
A 12-month period in which a business estimates revenues and budgets expenses.

1. Secure $150K in expansion capital.

2. Achieve cash flow self-sufficiency by the end of FISCAL YEAR (FY) 2.

3. Increase revenue from $1.5M in FY 2 to $5M by the end of FY 4.

Assignment #8: Develop Your Company's Objectives

Use the following pages to develop your company's short-term, mid-term and long-term objectives.

Objectives Worksheets

Tip! *Objectives answer **WHAT** you want to achieve.*

Short-Term Objectives

_____

_____

_____

_____

_____

_____

Mid-Term Objectives

_____

_____

_____

_____

_____

_____

Long-Term Objectives

_____

_____

_____

_____

_____

_____

My Company's Objectives

Identifying your objectives is the eighth step towards successful strategic business planning.

Critical Success Factors

***CRITICAL SUCCESS FACTORS** are the positive influences in the environment that impact your company's ability to achieve its mission, vision and objectives.*

A company cannot succeed independent of internal and external influences that positively impact the company. An example of an internal critical success factor is hiring good employees.

According to a CareerBuilder study[3], sixty-nine percent (69%) of employers reported that their companies have been adversely affected by a bad hire, with forty-one percent (41%) of those businesses estimating the cost to be over $25,000 and twenty-four percent (24%) reporting a bad hire cost them more than $50,000.

Hiring good employees is totally within the control of the company's leadership and it is a critical success factor that can and will impact a company's bottom line.

An example of an external critical success factor is the cost of fuel. A company that uses delivery or work vehicles may budget for fluctuations in fuel costs, but they have no control over those fluctuations. Even with fluctuations in price, the cost of fuel must remain within the amount budgeted, the critical success factor, in order for the company to earn a profit.

Other examples of critical success factors (CSF) include:

- ***The cost of capital (interest rate) on borrowed money INTERNAL AND EXTERNAL FACTOR.** The interest rate you pay on a loan is based, in part, your personal and business credit rating. Maintaining good credit rating is an internal CSF. On the other hand, a bank or lender sets interest rates based on a variety of factors that are out of the control of a borrower which means it is also an external CSF.*

- ***New contracts that yield 15% net profit on every project INTERNAL FACTOR.** Submitting a cost proposal for a project that includes a specific profit margin (in this case 15%) is determined by the company.*

- ***Completion of all projects on time or early INTERNAL AND EXTERNAL FACTOR.** The internal CSF includes the effective management of the company's resources. The external CSF might include the uncertainty of the weather.*

Assignment #9: Identify Your Company's Critical Success Factors

Use the following pages to identify the internal and external critical success factors that will impact your company's ability to achieve its mission, vision and objectives.

---

[3] Source: CareerBuilder.com (http://cb.com/TQC4dg)

Critical Success Factors Worksheets

Internal Critical Success Factors

_____

_____

_____

_____

_____

_____

_____

_____

_____

External Critical Success Factors

_____

_____

_____

_____

_____

_____

_____

_____

_____

_____

My Company's Critical Success Factors

_____
_____
_____
_____
_____
_____
_____
_____
_____
_____
_____
_____
_____
_____
_____
_____
_____
_____

Identifying the internal and external critical success factors that impact your company is the ninth step towards successful strategic business planning.

Strategies

*The word **STRATEGY** is from the Greek word strategos which means "leader" or "general".*

From the days of the ancient Greeks to today's modern armies, strategy has referred to the coordination, planning and execution of warfare. In a business context, strategy is the coordination, planning and execution of your business.

In short, business strategies explain how your company will achieve its objectives.

If your objective is to reach annual sales of $5 million by the end of your second year, your strategies might include...

Strategy #1: *Develop a funding proposal to present to bankers and investors.*

Assumption: *The business will need an infusion of capital to grow and meet its objectives.*

Strategy #2: Implement financial controls to monitor revenues and expenses.

Assumption: Monitoring revenues and controlling costs can help maximize profitability.

Strategy #3: Launch a national marketing campaign to improve brand awareness.

Assumption: Improving brand awareness can lead to an increase in sales.

Strategies are formulated to generate results. In order to generate the results you desire, your strategies must be aligned with your idea, your business model, your mission and all of the steps previously discussed.

Assignment #10: Formulating Your Company's Strategies

Use the following pages to formulate your company's strategies. Refer to your idea and all of the other components of your *One Page Strategic Business Plan* listed below to ensure your strategies align with your overall plan.

IDEA	BUSINESS MODEL	MASTER MIND GROUP
MISSION	VISION	VALUES
SWOT	OBJECTIVES	CRITICAL SUCCESS FACTORS

Strategies Worksheets

*Tip! Strategies answer **HOW** you are going to achieve your objectives.*

Strategy:_____

_____

_____

_____

Strategy:_____

_____

_____

_____

Strategy:_____

_____

_____

_____

Strategy:_____

_____

_____

_____

Strategy:_____

_____

_____

_____

ULTIMATE STRATEGY
HOW TO WRITE A ONE PAGE STRATEGIC BUSINESS PLAN

Strategy:_____

_____

_____

_____

Strategy:_____

_____

_____

_____

Strategy:_____

_____

_____

_____

Strategy:_____

_____

_____

_____

Strategy:_____

_____

_____

_____

My Company's Strategies

_____
_____
_____
_____
_____
_____
_____
_____
_____
_____
_____
_____
_____
_____
_____
_____
_____
_____
_____
_____
_____

Formulating your strategies is the tenth step towards
successful strategic business planning.

Prioritized Action Plan

*A **PRIORITIZED ACTION PLAN** includes specific tasks assigned to owners, employees or other "key players" that must be completed for a company to achieve its vision.*

Also known as milestones in a business plan, a prioritized action plan defines roles and responsibilities and holds individuals accountable for successes and failures for tasks that are critical to the success of the business. Your prioritized action plan lists tasks in order from the first action that needs to be completed to the last.

Sample Prioritized Action Plans (Narrative Format)

1. The chief executive officer (CEO) will complete a One Page Strategic Business Plan in 30-days.

2. The CEO and chief operating officer (COO) will complete a business plan in 60-days.

3. The chief financial officer (CFO) will complete a funding proposal for investors in 90-days.

4. The chief marketing officer (CMO) and chief information officer (CIO) will develop a national radio, TV and internet advertising campaign in 120-days.

Sample Prioritized Action Plans (Table Format)

Task	Start Date	Completion Date	By
Complete our One Page Strategic Business Plan	06/01/2016	06/30/2016	CEO
Complete our business plan	07/01/2016	08/31/2016	CEO; COO
Prepare a funding proposal for investors	09/01/2016	11/30/2016	CFO
Develop a national radio, TV and internet ad campaign	10/01/2016	01/31/2017	CMO; CIO

Assignment #11: Create Your Company's Prioritized Action Plan

Use the following pages to create your company's prioritized action plan.

Prioritized Action Plan Worksheets

Task Description: _____

_____

_____

Task #: _____ | Time allotted to complete[4]: _____ | Start date: _____ | End date: _____

Assigned To: _____

Task Description: _____

_____

_____

Task #: _____ | Time allotted to complete: _____ | Start date: _____ | End date: _____

Assigned To: _____

Task Description: _____

_____

_____

Task #: _____ | Time allotted to complete: _____ | Start date: _____ | End date: _____

Assigned To: _____

Task Description: _____

_____

_____

Task #: _____ | Time allotted to complete: _____ | Start date: _____ | End date: _____

Assigned To: _____

---

[4] For example, number of days, weeks, months or years.

ULTIMATE STRATEGY

How to Write a One Page Strategic Business Plan

Task Description: _____

_____

_____

Task #: _____ | Time allotted to complete: _____ | Start date: _____ | End date: _____

Assigned To: _____

Task Description: _____

_____

_____

Task #: _____ | Time allotted to complete: _____ | Start date: _____ | End date: _____

Assigned To: _____

Task Description: _____

_____

_____

Task #: _____ | Time allotted to complete: _____ | Start date: _____ | End date: _____

Assigned To: _____

Task Description: _____

_____

_____

Task #: _____ | Time allotted to complete: _____ | Start date: _____ | End date: _____

Assigned To: _____

My Company's Prioritized Action Plan

Task Description: _____

_____

_____

Task #: _____ | Time allotted to complete: _____ | Start date: _____ | End date: _____

Assigned To: _____

Task Description: _____

_____

_____

Task #: _____ | Time allotted to complete: _____ | Start date: _____ | End date: _____

Assigned To: _____

Task Description: _____

_____

_____

Task #: _____ | Time allotted to complete: _____ | Start date: _____ | End date: _____

Assigned To: _____

Task Description: _____

_____

_____

Task #: _____ | Time allotted to complete: _____ | Start date: _____ | End date: _____

Assigned To: _____

My Company's Prioritized Action Plan (Continued)

Task Description: _____

_____

_____

Task #: _____ | Time allotted to complete: _____ | Start date: _____ | End date: _____

Assigned To: _____

Task Description: _____

_____

_____

Task #: _____ | Time allotted to complete: _____ | Start date: _____ | End date: _____

Assigned To: _____

Task Description: _____

_____

_____

Task #: _____ | Time allotted to complete: _____ | Start date: _____ | End date: _____

Assigned To: _____

Task Description: _____

_____

_____

Task #: _____ | Time allotted to complete: _____ | Start date: _____ | End date: _____

Assigned To: _____

Creating your prioritized action plan is the eleventh step towards successful strategic business planning.

Writing Your One Page Strategic Business Plan

The final step is to put all the elements of your plan together into a single one page strategic business plan. Trust me when I say it can be done in one page, and to prove it, I have included a few sample plans beginning on page 51.

However, if you must, use a second page to ensure all of the elements of your plan are included in your strategic business plan. If you go beyond two pages, your strategic business plan is probably too wordy and may not be well-received by potential banks or investors.

Keep in mind that you can attach pictures of your products or services, a brief start-up cost table, or a financial projections summary to your one page strategic business plan without exceeding the one, or two page, narrative limit.

Putting Your Plans into Action

The world we live in changes every second of every minute of every day. What that means is that all of the planning in the world cannot guarantee business success. Your plans require continuous re-evaluation to ensure the plans you had yesterday will help you achieve success today, tomorrow and beyond. Most importantly, you must put your plans into action in order to achieve success.

To improve your chances for long-term business success, put your one page strategic business plan in a place where you can see it and read it every day. Read it every morning and commit it to memory to the point that every action you take in business revolves around achieving the plans you outlined in your one page strategic business plan.

Next, ask yourself three questions every day:

When you awake in the morning ask yourself:
WHAT CAN I DO TODAY TOWARDS ACHIEVING MY GOALS?

Every day at noon ask yourself:
AM I DOING WHAT I NEED TO DO TODAY TOWARDS ACHIEVING MY GOALS?

Before you go to sleep every night ask yourself:
DID I DO EVERYTHING POSSIBLE TODAY TOWARDS ACHIEVING MY GOALS?

Putting your plans into action is the twelfth and final step towards successful strategic business planning.

Sample One Page Strategic Business Plans

ACE Consulting

Mission Statement	ACE Consulting is an information technology (IT) company dedicated to providing high-quality cloud computer network services to medium-sized corporations and local government agencies. ACE Consulting strives to provide the best hardware and software solutions for our clients and to be a value-added partner to our clients.
Vision Statement	Within the first three (3) years of operations, grow ACE Consulting into a $12.5 million dollar national IT consulting company.
Values Statement	ACE Consulting is committed to acting honestly and ethically in all our dealings and we are committed to treating our employees, clients and partners fairly.

Competitive Analysis	
Strengths	Highly qualified management team. High profit margin across product and service lines.
Weaknesses	Limited access to capital. Too much dependence on the Chief Information Officer.
Opportunities	Partnerships with global IT companies. Corporate IT network upgrades.
Threats	Potential entry of new competitors. In-house IT management.
Objectives	- Secure fifty (50) new clients in the first 12-months of operations. - Achieve cash flow self-sufficiency by the end of Fiscal Year 2. - Increase revenue from $1.5M in FY 1 to $12.5M by the end of FY 3.
Critical Success Factors	- Repeat business with 50% of our corporate and government clients. - Maintain a cost of goods sold at or below 20% of overall project cost. - Lead generating website that provides 25% of new business annually.
Strategies	- Secure $150,000 in expansion capital. - Secure certified IT developer/operator status with three (3) global IT firms. - Launch a national ad campaign to improve brand awareness.
Prioritized Action Plan	1. **Complete funding plan and proposal.** Chief Financial Officer (CFO) to complete the task within 15-days. 2. **Secure $150K in expansion capital.** Chief Executive Officer (CEO) and CFO to complete task in 60-days. 3. **Hire advertising and public relations firms.** Marketing Director and CEO to complete task in 90-days

Integrated Contractors

Mission Statement	Integrated Contractors is dedicated to offering the finest residential construction and renovation services to residential real estate developers and homeowners. We maintain the highest standards of quality in the residential construction industry and we always strive to exceed the expectations of our clients.
Vision Statement	By 2016, grow Integrated Contractors into a leading provider of residential construction and renovation services in the Springfield metro area.
Values Statement	Quality, value and service are the standards by which operate. Additionally, Integrated Contractors always acts responsibly in the communities where we work.
Competitive Analysis	
Strengths	Forty (40) years of experience in the construction industry. Low overhead costs.
Weaknesses	Inexperienced field supervisors. Limited access to credit lines for materials.
Opportunities	Government contracting. Capitalize on emerging technologies like solar power.
Threats	Competition from larger construction firms. New, more stringent mortgage regulations.
Objectives	- Secure $2.5 million in government contracts in FY 1. - Contract with three (3) new residential developer clients by the end of Fiscal Year 2. - Increase profit margin from 12% to 17% per project by the end of FY 2.
Critical Success Factors	- Stability in mortgage interest rates for the next 36-months. - Annual inflation rate on construction materials under 5%.
Strategies	- Secure an unsecured line of credit to improve cash flow management. - Invest in a state-of-the-industry estimating software program to maximize profitability. - Secure small business enterprise (SBE) certification to increase access to government contracting opportunities.
Prioritized Action Plan	1. **Complete line of credit funding application package.** Chief Financial Officer (CFO) to complete the task within 15-days. 2. **Secure $150K in credit lines with suppliers.** Chief Executive Officer (CEO) and CFO to complete task in 60-days. 3. **Purchase new estimating software program and train staff.** Construction supervisor to complete task in 90-days. 4. **Complete SBE certification application.** Chief Operating Officer (COO) to complete task in 120-days.

ABC Company

Mission Statement	Our mission is to provide entrepreneurs with the knowledge and skills they need to succeed through workshops, books, videos and audio books.
Vision Statement	Our vision is to become a global consulting and training company by 2016.
Corporate Values Statement	Ethical, honest, trustworthy, respectful and responsible are the values by which we operate. As a result, ABC Company will engage in no transaction that does not benefit all parties involved.

Competitive Analysis	
Strengths	Quality products, great brand and our track record of success.
Weaknesses	Ineffective marketing strategy and a lack of production scalability.
Opportunities	Multi-level marketing sales channels and affiliate sales programs.
Threats	No patent and limited copyright protection.
Objectives	- Sale of 5,000 seminar and workshop seats in the first 180-days. - Sale of 25,000 books, videos and audio books in FY 2. - Revenue of $2.5M by the end of FY 3.
Critical Success Factors	- Adequate capital and cash flow to support operations through the first 24-months. - Achieve and maintain a 5 to 1 mark-up on all products and services. - Achieve and maintain a website conversion rate above 5%.
Strategies	- Secure $15,000 in start-up capital for product development, website development and internet radio test marketing campaign. - Develop a single product website with an intelligent branching shopping cart and a high conversion rate for product sales. - Develop an affiliate program that brings in incremental orders. - Hire an order fulfillment company to supplement to website sales. - Cross-sell through online e-book stores Amazon Kindle and B&N Nook.
Prioritized Action Plan	1. Complete loan package and secure capital by August 1st (15-days) 2. Finalize first two (2) book and video products by August 15th (30-days) 3. Develop radio 30- and 60-second radio ads by August 30th (45-days) 4. Launch website and radio ad campaign by August 30th (45-days) 5. Launch direct marketing ad campaign by September 1st (47-days)

Sample Mission Statements

Company	Mission
Bank of New York	We strive to be the acknowledged global leader and preferred partner in helping our clients succeed in the world's rapidly evolving financial markets.
Starbucks	Our mission is to inspire and nurture the human spirit – one person, one cup and one neighborhood at a time.
Citigroup	Our goal for Citigroup is to be the most respected global financial services company. Like any other public company, we're obligated to deliver profits and growth to our shareholders. Of equal importance is to deliver those profits and generate growth responsibly.
FedEx	FedEx will produce superior financial returns for shareowners by providing high value-added supply chain, transportation, business and related information services through focused operating companies. Customer requirements will be met in the highest quality manner appropriate to each market segment served. FedEx will strive to develop mutually rewarding relationships with its employees, partners and suppliers. Safety will be the first consideration in all operations. Corporate activities will be conducted to the highest ethical and professional standards.
Ford Motor Co.	We are a global family with a proud heritage passionately committed to providing personal mobility for people around the world.
Nike	To Bring Inspiration and innovation to every athlete in the world.
Google	Google's mission is to organize the world's information and make it universally accessible and useful.
MetLife	The capable team of MetLife's Customer Response Center shares a common mission - that all customers are "Met for Life." By balancing the efficiencies of new technologies with the personal touch of highly trained and motivated professionals, we are able to deliver solutions and services that exceed our customers' expectations. We thereby earn their loyalty.
Capital Access Project, Inc.	Capital Access Project is dedicated to supporting the creation of competitively viable small, disadvantaged, minority, and women-owned firms through business development assistance by identifying, qualifying, and matching those firms with public and private sector capital and resources to start or expand their businesses, create jobs, and create an economic impact that would otherwise not exist without our efforts.

Sample Vision Statements

Company	Vision
Coca Cola	To achieve sustainable growth, we have established a vision with clear goals. - Profit: Maximizing return to shareowners while being mindful of our overall responsibilities. - People: Being a great place to work where people are inspired to be the best they can be. - Portfolio: Bringing to the world a portfolio of beverage brands that anticipate and satisfy people's desires and needs. - Partners: Nurturing a winning network of partners and building mutual loyalty. - Planet: Being a responsible global citizen that makes a difference.
McDonald's	McDonald's vision is to be the world's best quick service restaurant experience. Being the best means providing outstanding quality, service, cleanliness, and value, so that we make every customer in every restaurant smile.
Toyota	Innovation into the Future - A Passion to Create a Better Society. Through "Monozukuri - manufacturing of value - added products" and "technological innovation," Toyota is helping to create a more prosperous society.
General Motors	GM's vision is to be the world leader in transportation products and related services. We will earn our customers' enthusiasm through continuous improvement driven by the integrity, teamwork, and innovation of GM people.

Perform an internet search for **mission statements**, **vision statements** or any other strategic business planning topic to find more examples and guidance from successful companies.

Sample Objectives and Strategies

Sample Objectives	Sample Strategies
• Increase market share • Achieve $X,XXX,XXX in sales • Achieve $X,XXX,XXX in profit • Achieve a XX% increase in sales • Achieve a XX% increase in profits • Build a better product than our competitors • Maximize customer satisfaction • Reduce overhead expenses • Maintain cost controls • Maximize revenue opportunities • Maximize gross profit • Maximize profit • Maximize net profit • Maximize shareholder value • Maximize return on investment (ROI) • Maximize return on equity (ROE) • Maximize return on assets (ROA) • Maximize return on sales (ROS) • Expand into new markets • Expand internationally	• Build a track record of success through excellent customer service. • Build a competitive advantage by maintaining cost controls. • Focus growth efforts by building a regional client base. • Use press releases and word-of-mouth referrals as a primary marketing strategy. • Build brand awareness by participating in trade shows. • Build company awareness through local networking groups and professional organizations. • Develop products in-house to maintain quality control. • Increase efficiency by developing convertible product templates. • Increase potential revenue by bundling products and/or services. • Outsource sales staff to reduce expenses. • Develop relationships with major supplier to improve credit terms.

Other Products by Norman David Roussell

ULTIMATE PLANNING

THE ULTIMATE BUSINESS PLAN PLANNER

✓ Get unmatched insight and expert guidance on writing the ultimate business plan using our examples and worksheets for every component of a bank or investor-ready business plan

✓ Learn the keys to ultimate business planning and tap into the resources that will power your long-term success and growth in business

✓ Learn how to evaluate your business plan and make critical improvements to it before you apply for a loan or approach investors

✓ Learn proven and creative financing strategies and tips to raise the capital you need to start or grow your business

N O R M A N   D A V I D   R O U S S E L L ,   M B A

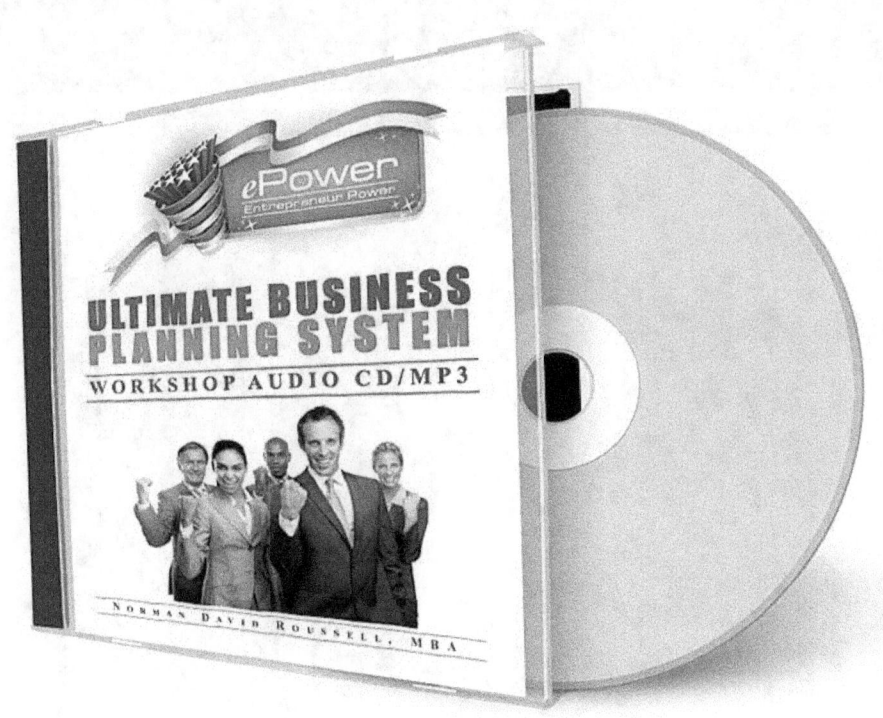